P9-CML-299

WEST GA REG LIB SYS
Neva Lomason
Memorial Library

Energy Alternatives

Robert Snedden

Heinemann Library
Chicago, Illinois

© 2002 Reed Educational & Professional Publishing
Published by Heinemann Library,
an imprint of Reed Educational & Professional Publishing,
Chicago, Illinois

Customer Service 888-454-2279

Visit our website at www.heinemannlibrary.com

All rights reserved. No part of this publication may be reproduced or transmitted in any form or by any means, electronic or mechanical, including photocopying, recording, taping, or any information storage and retrieval system, without permission in writing from the publisher.

Text and cover designed by Celia Floyd
Illustrated by Jeff Edwards and Alan Fraser
Originated by Ambassador Litho Ltd.
Printed in Hong Kong by Wing King Tong

06 05 04 03 02
10 9 8 7 6 5 4 3 2 1

Library of Congress Cataloging-in-Publication Data

Snedden, Robert.
  Energy alternatives / by Robert Snedden.
      p. cm. -- (Essential energy)
Includes bibliographical references and index.
  ISBN 1-57572-441-3 (lib. bdg.)
  1. Power resources--Juvenile literature. 2. Renewable energy
sources--Juvenile literature. [1. Power resources. 2. Renewable energy
sources.] I. Title.
  TJ163.23 .S675 2001
  333.79--dc21
                                    00-013237

Acknowledgments
The author and publishers are grateful to the following for permission to reproduce copyright material:
Science Photo Library, pp.4, 7, 16, 17, 20, 25, 30, 39, 40; Corbis, pp.5, 6, 26, 28, 32, 36, 38, 41; United States Environmental Protection Agency, p.11; Environmental Images, pp.12, 15, 19, 27, 29, 31; Popperfoto, pp.13, 33, 42; Ginny Stroud Lewis, p.21; Empics, p.23; Camera Press, p.24; South American Pictures, p.34; Still Pictures, p.35.

Cover photograph reproduced with permission of Environmental Images.

Every effort has been made to contact copyright holders of any material reproduced in this book. Any omissions will be rectified in subsequent printings if notice is given to the publisher.

Some words are shown in bold, **like this.** You can find out what they mean by looking in the glossary.

Contents

Today's Questions, Tomorrow's Answers?

When the world had a plentiful supply of **fossil fuels,** there seemed to be little need to look for alternative energy sources. Many people thought that alternative energy technologies were something that could be developed in the distant future. However, people are realizing that now is the time to come up with the solutions.

Oil crisis

In 1973, the world was shaken when **OPEC,** the Organization of **Petroleum** Exporting Countries, quadrupled the price of oil. The United States, Europe, and most of the rest of the world were faced

This coal-fired power station is in Germany. Pollution problems and shrinking resources mean alternatives will have to be found.

with an energy crisis. People started thinking about alternative energy sources. The U.S. Congress established the **Solar Energy** Research Institute (SERI), and breakthroughs were made in developing solar-energy technology. President Jimmy Carter even installed a water-heating solar-energy panel at the White House.

However, the energy crisis passed after OPEC members increased oil production, and fuel supplies began to flow again. As oil prices fell, so did interest in energy conservation and alternative energy. In 1981, the U.S. government cut SERI's funding almost by half. Alternative energy was pushed aside in favor of **nuclear energy** and developing fossil fuel sources. In 2000, energy made headlines again as high fuel prices angered **consumers.**

Looking for alternatives

Today, we are more aware of the need to find energy alternatives. Not only are fossil fuels a dwindling resource, but they also cause such environmental damage as smog, **acid rain, global warming,** and oil spills. Nuclear power, which was once seen as an answer to our energy problems, has its own risks. The disposal of dangerous nuclear waste and the risk of accidents such as the one in Chernobyl, Ukraine, has led many people to question the safety of nuclear power.

There can be no doubt that we need to cut down on the use of fossil fuels. The good news is that there are alternatives. Solar power is one alternative. Another is wind power, which has been used for centuries to drive windmills. Today, wind power can be harnessed to generate more electricity using wind **turbines.** Ocean waves and tides can be used to drive **generators** that produce electricity. In other energy alternatives, animal and plant wastes can be processed to produce **natural gas.** This **biomass** energy is widely used in many parts of the world. **Geothermal energy** comes from the hot rock inside Earth. In places such as Iceland and New Zealand, it is used to generate electricity and to heat buildings. **Hydroelectricity,** which was once thought to be a clean way of producing power, is less popular now because of the damage that building dams can do to the environment.

An erupting geyser is evidence of the powerful geothermal energy beneath Earth's surface.

Why Do We Need Energy?

We cannot see energy with our eyes, but we can see what it does. The warmth of a summer's day is caused by energy traveling from the Sun through 93 million miles (150 million kilometers) of space. You cannot see the heat, but you can feel it. When you throw a ball, food energy stored as chemicals in your muscles becomes the energy of movement in the ball. You cannot see that change taking place, either. You cannot see the energy that makes the ball move.

Work and energy

Energy makes things happen. Without energy, everything would stop. Science defines the term *energy* as "the ability to do work." Work is the transfer of energy from one place to another. When you threw that ball, you were doing work!

Energy cannot be created or destroyed, but it can be changed into different forms. The energy stored in your muscles is **chemical energy.** The energy of movement that you gave the ball is **kinetic energy.** When the ball hits the ground, its vibration will cause air particles to vibrate, changing kinetic energy into sound energy. Fast movement generates heat called **heat energy.**

As a ball is thrown, the chemical energy in the player's muscles is turned into the kinetic energy of the ball.

Energy resources

Most of our energy, except for **nuclear** and **geothermal energy,** comes from the Sun. Inside the Sun, under enormous pressures and temperatures, hydrogen **atoms** join together and become helium. This process, called **nuclear fusion,** gives off large amounts of energy. The energy goes out into space to reach Earth as heat and light. Plants change this **solar energy** into chemical energy, and animals eat them to get their stored chemical energy.

The energy stored in **fossil fuels** also came from the Sun. Fossil fuels are the remains of plants and animals that lived millions of years ago. After the plants and animals died, they were covered with layers of sediment year after year. After millions of years, they turned into coal and **petroleum.** Today, when we burn fossil fuels, we are releasing stored energy from the Sun.

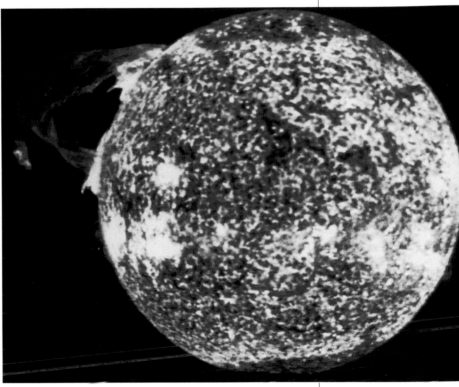

The Sun is the ultimate source of most of the energy we use.

Renewable energy

Fossil fuels supply most of our energy needs. However, fossil fuels are nonrenewable sources of energy. This means that the amount of fossil fuel available is limited, and one day will run out. Scientists are trying to find sources of **renewable energy** that can be used in place of fossil fuels. Even though several energy sources look promising, none seem to be as useful or as convenient to use as fossil fuels. During the summer of 2000, our heavy dependence on fossil fuels was made clear when prices soared. Around the world, motorists complained loudly and governments conducted investigations of oil companies.

Energy Efficiency

Before we study different alternative sources of energy, it helps to see how we are making use of the energy we have available now. One way to limit the energy problem is to use the energy sources we have more efficiently and to cut down on waste.

Measuring efficiency

There are several ways to measure how efficiently we use our energy resources. Efficiency is measured in terms of output, or how much work is done, compared to the input, or how much energy went into making and running the machine. This comparison is usually expressed as a percentage. Some energy is lost in every process, so nothing is ever 100 percent efficient. However, a better design can often increase the efficiency of a machine or process. The more efficient a machine or process is, the more of our energy resources we will conserve.

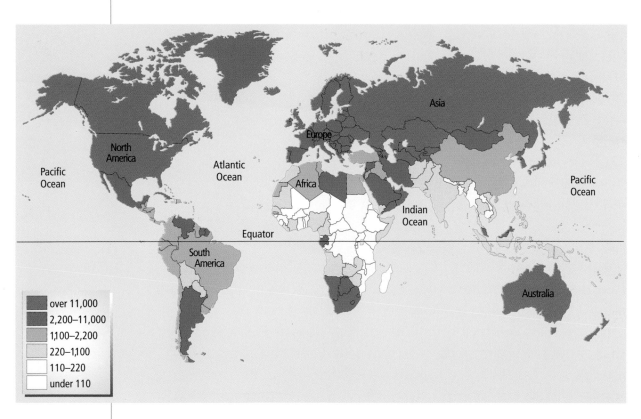

Energy consumption across the world is shown here in pounds of coal per person. In kilograms, these levels would be: more than 5,000; 1,000–5,000; 500–1,000; 100–500; 50–100; and under 50.

Energy consumption

Four sets of factors, or criteria, determine how much energy is used in a society:

Population and geography: A big country with a cold climate and a lot of people will tend to use more energy than a small country where the weather is mild.

Economic factors: Although there is no direct link between a nation's wealth and energy use, higher-income countries with more industry do use more energy than poorer countries with less industry.

Technological factors: These determine how efficiently machines use energy.

Lifestyles: Our lifestyle includes a variety of energy-related factors. For example, we can choose whether or not to live in smaller houses, buy more efficient cars, **recycle** as much as possible, and use public transportation.

Energy use

We use a lot of energy to heat our homes and workplaces in winter and to cool them in summer. We use electricity to light our towns and cities and to operate our televisions, radios, computers, refrigerators, washing machines, and other gadgets. Most of this electricity is produced by burning **fossil fuels,** which are a convenient source of energy.

Fossil fuel energy powers our cars and other vehicles. Today's cars are much more energy-efficient than they were twenty years ago, and will travel a lot further on a tank of gasoline. However, there are now many more cars on the road, and people drive more frequently than they did in the past.

Factories use energy to make all the goods we, as **consumers,** demand, including preparing and packaging the food we eat, the clothes we wear, the furniture in our homes, the books we read, and the games we play.

Making plastics uses up a lot of our fossil fuel reserves. Not only are plastics made from oil, but they use fossil fuels for the energy required in the manufacturing process. What's even worse is that many plastic products are designed to be used once and then thrown away.

Home Economics

As home-buyers become aware of the costs of energy and the damage it does to the environment through pollution and **global warming,** more and more of them are looking for energy-efficient homes. After all, energy efficiency does not just save the environment, it saves money, too.

There are many things we can all do to save energy. Using **insulation** in roofs and in wall cavities has a huge impact on how much energy we use. Up to 40 percent of the heating in a home can escape through the ceiling. Double-paned windows also help save energy. The thermostat controls on radiators, furnaces, and hot-water heaters help, too. A simple way to save energy is to set radiator thermostats so they cannot be put above a certain temperature, such as 68° F (23° C). Putting on warmer clothing on a cold day could mean not having to turn up the heat.

You can help save electricity by remembering to turn off all the lights when you leave a room. Replacing ordinary light bulbs with energy-saving bulbs, sometimes called compact fluorescent lights, will save more energy. These bulbs use only about 25 percent of the energy that normal light bulbs use, and they last around eight times longer. It also helps to turn off radios, televisions, and computers whenever they are not being used.

Effective insulation can lower a homeowner's energy costs dramatically.

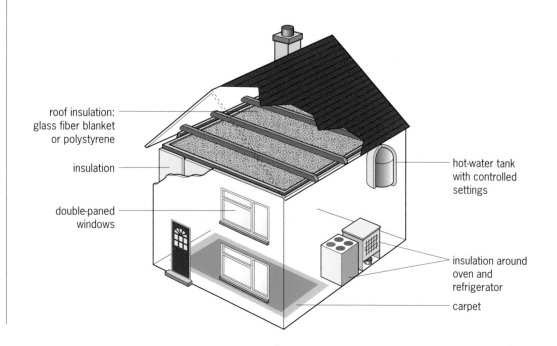

roof insulation: glass fiber blanket or polystyrene

insulation

double-paned windows

hot-water tank with controlled settings

insulation around oven and refrigerator

carpet

Recycle and save

Everyone should **recycle** newspapers because paper made from recycled paper uses about one-third less energy than paper made from raw materials. Making glass from recycled bottles also uses about one-third less energy than making glass from raw materials. Recycling steel and aluminum cans and aluminum foil is also very energy efficient. It takes 90 percent less energy to make an aluminum can from recycled materials than it does to make one using raw materials.

Energy Star

The Energy Star program has been set up jointly by the United States Environmental Protection Agency and Department of Energy to promote the use of energy-efficient products. Products are awarded an Energy Star label if they meet or exceed the minimum standards set by the program. There are more than 3,000 Energy Star products, which include light bulbs that burn brighter for longer, and washing machines that use up to 60 percent less energy than average appliances. The European Union is also interested in strengthening existing energy-efficiency labeling programs. It recommends setting efficiency standards for appliances such as water heaters, air conditioners, dishwashers, electric motors, pumps, and commercial refrigeration equipment.

Money Isn't All You're Saving

The energy star on packaging assures **consumers** that they are buying an energy-efficient product.

Transportation Technology

There are more cars and other vehicles on our roads than there have ever been before, and the numbers show no signs of decreasing. Like other aspects of alternative energy, the enthusiasm for developing transportation alternatives seems to rise and fall with oil prices. Falling oil prices seem to encourage people to drive four-wheel-drive vehicles known for their low gas-mileage. So what alternative forms of transportation can we look into, now and in the future, to conserve energy?

Cutting down on carbon dioxide

In industrialized countries, such as those in North America and Europe, transportation accounts for around 30 percent of energy usage and more than 80 percent of carbon dioxide emissions. This is a serious problem, because carbon dioxide is a **greenhouse gas** strongly believed by many to be contributing to the overall warming of Earth. This warming is believed to create dangerous changes in the global climate.

It is obvious that there are many ways to save energy. To cut down on gasoline consumption, we could all walk or ride bicycles a little more often rather than driving everywhere. For longer trips, people could take the bus or train instead. In many places, however, public transportation is poor. It will have to be improved to convince motorists to change their ways.

Cars use large amounts of gasoline. Vehicle exhaust is a major source of pollution, as seen here on the Santa Monica Freeway in Los Angeles, California.

Petroleum substitutes

Gasoline and other **petroleum**-based fuels supply nearly all the energy that powers the world's transportation systems. It is vital to conserve fuel, not only because of the threat of a serious fuel shortage, but also because of the high cost of pollution.

More than half the energy used for transportation in the industrialized nations is used by cars. Governments can try to encourage car manufacturers to produce smaller, lighter, and more fuel-efficient cars. Eventually, however, we will need to find substitutes for petroleum fuels. Already there are companies producing **synthetic** liquid fuels from coal, **natural gas, biomass,** oil shale, and bituminous sands—which are sands containing bitumen, a substance in which oil can be found. A fuel called **ethanol,** or ethyl alcohol, is made from sugar-cane pulp or corn.

Sun racers

A race called the World Solar Challenge is held every three years. In the 1999 race, 40 solar-powered cars lined up to race 1,860 miles (3,000 kilometers) across Australia from Darwin to Adelaide. One of the most important aspects of the Solar Challenge is to demonstrate how alternative energy sources can provide a more environmentally friendly form of transportation.

This odd-looking vehicle was one of the entries in the 1996 World Solar Challenge.

Batteries Not Included

Another way to cut down on our dependence on **fossil fuel** would be to use electric motors to power vehicles. During the 1980s and early 1990s, battery-powered cars were seen as the answer to vehicle pollution and fuel shortages. Regulations in California, New York, and Massachusetts even required that two percent of the 1998-model vehicles produced by the seven largest car manufacturers ran on electricity. However, electric cars have not been popular with **consumers.**

Electric vehicles

The first mass-produced electric vehicle was General Motors' EV1. Two years after it came on the market at the end of 1996, just over 500 had been sold. By 1999, scarcely more than 2,000 electric vehicles had been sold or leased in the United States. Compare this to the eight million new vehicles General Motors alone sells in the United States each year.

Against electric

There are several reasons that electric cars have not sold very well. First, they cost $30,000, or more. Second, they can only cover about 60 miles (100 kilometers) before they have to be recharged. A gasoline-powered car can travel four or five times farther using a tank of gasoline. There are also few places along the road where people can plug in their rechargers. It takes four to eight hours to recharge an electric vehicle's battery. It only takes about five minutes to refill a gasoline tank.

Hybrids

One type of vehicle avoids some of the problems posed by electric cars. **Hybrid** vehicles combine electricity with **internal combustion engines.** Hybrids use small diesel engines or gas **turbines** that act as on-board **generators** to recharge the batteries, therefore extending the vehicle's range. The hybrid uses a nickel-metal-**hydride** battery pack designed specifically for use in hybrid vehicles.

General Motors has produced a hybrid electric vehicle that uses a 137-horsepower electric motor for power and a small gas turbine that acts as a generator to keep the battery pack charged. This hybrid should have a range of nearly 375 miles (600 kilometers) with a top speed of 80 miles (130 kilometers) per hour. It also causes much less pollution than a car using a regular internal combustion engine.

Computer controlled

Production costs remain one of the greatest potential problems for electric vehicles and hybrids. Hybrids need more sophisticated control systems than ordinary cars do. A hybrid vehicle's fuel efficiency can be cut dramatically under real driving conditions. Air conditioners, windshield wipers, heaters, defoggers, defrosters, and headlights all drain power from the battery. Bad weather and the stop-and-go driving conditions of towns and cities can lower the fuel economy even more.

New computer systems would allow the hybrid vehicles to adjust to the weather, traffic, and a driver's habits. Sophisticated control systems would adapt to the driver, learning how hard he or she accelerates and brakes. Hybrids are well-suited for such techniques because they can store energy for later use. Conventional vehicles, on the other hand, waste energy when braking. Hybrids use their internal combustion engines only as a way to store charge in the batteries, not to provide a driving force. Electrical current passes to the electric motor by the control system only as it is needed.

Some environmentalists remain optimistic about electric cars. The nickel-metal-hydride batteries currently being developed will double the distance that could be covered by the lead-acid batteries used in the EV1. However, many people see another type of vehicle as far more promising.

The battery in an electric car has to be recharged, as seen here.

Fuel Cells

This is how the fuel cell inside Europe's first hydrogen-powered taxi looked.

Fuel cells appear to be the ideal solution to many of our energy problems. They generate electricity by combining hydrogen and oxygen, producing water as a harmless waste product. Unlike a battery, the reacting chemicals are not stored inside the cell. They are supplied from the outside, and the waste products are removed. Car manufacturers are spending large sums of money to develop fuel cells. Many energy experts believe that hydrogen gas could one day become an environmentally friendly replacement for **fossil fuels.**

Hydrogen sources

The biggest problem in developing fuel cells is finding a source of hydrogen. One way might be to split water into hydrogen and oxygen by electrolysis, but this itself requires energy. An alternative involves taking hydrogen from the type of hydrocarbon **molecules** found in fossil fuels. However, this process produces carbon dioxide, a **greenhouse gas**, as a by-product.

The best results—that is, the greatest amount of hydrogen that can be produced for the least amount of carbon dioxide—come from processing methane, the main ingredient of **natural gas.** Every methane molecule is made up of one carbon and four hydrogen **atoms**—the best balance of hydrogen and carbon that is possible. Natural gas is also cheap and easy to reform into hydrogen and carbon dioxide. Scientists believe that a car running on a fuel cell that uses methane to get its hydrogen would be no more expensive to run than a car using unleaded gasoline. Of course, natural gas is a fossil fuel, and is in limited supply. However, it can be produced from biological wastes.

Another problem with natural gas is that it takes up a lot of space, even when it is compressed or turned into liquid. This could mean that natural gas would be used only in vehicles with the capacity to carry a large amount of fuel, such as trucks and buses.

One possible solution is to remove the hydrogen from large vessels at filling stations and then store it on vehicles in solids known as metal **hydrides.** A Detroit, Michigan, firm named Energy Conversion Devices has developed a device that can soak up hydrogen so well that a tank of hydride can deliver as much energy as a tank of gas the same size.

Hydrogen and algae

U.S. scientists have recently discovered an alga, a type of simple plant, that produces hydrogen. The researchers first grow the alga under normal conditions, allowing the **microorganisms** to collect sunlight and make carbohydrates through **photosynthesis.** When enough energy has been stored in this way, the alga is transferred into bottles free of sulfur—a chemical needed for photosynthesis.

By turning off the alga's ability to photosynthesize, the scientists force it to switch to another way of generating energy. This makes the alga produce hydrogen. After up to four days of generating hydrogen, the alga has used up its stored fuel and must be allowed to return to photosynthesis. Then, two or three days later, it can be used to produce hydrogen again.

Apollo 11 lifts off on its way to the Moon in 1969. Fuel cells provided the electrical power for the spacecraft.

Cogeneration

Industrial nations such as the United States, Britain, and France throw away as much energy in the form of waste heat from electricity production as they get from **natural gas**. A combination of heat and power called **cogeneration** uses the waste heat from electricity generation to heat homes and factories close to the power station. Cogeneration is not a new idea. In fact, the first power plant built by Thomas Edison in 1881 was run by cogeneration.

The electricity output from a cogeneration plant is lower than that of a conventional station. However, cogeneration uses waste heat far more effectively than conventional stations do. A cogeneration plant may change 80 percent of the original fuel energy into a mix of electricity and useful heat, while a conventional power station rarely changes even 40 percent.

Hot water from the cogeneration plant is pumped through **insulated** pipes into the heating systems of buildings nearby. In a way, the buildings being heated are taking the place of the conventional power station's cooling towers. The low cost of the heat makes this the cheapest method available of providing warmth for towns and cities.

About 50 percent of buildings in Denmark and Finland are heated from cogeneration plants, which provide a third of the electricity in those countries. In other European countries, ten to fifteen percent of electricity is provided by cogeneration plants. In the United States, that number is only ten percent.

Cogeneration and biofuel

In Scandinavia, cogeneration plants have been made more energy efficient and environmentally friendly. One Swedish company has built a **biofuel** pellet manufacturing facility at its cogeneration plant. The company can produce a high-energy biofuel using **heat energy** from the cogeneration plant. The plant has an output of approximately 63 megawatts of heat and 35 megawatts of electricity. When heat requirements are high during winter, only electricity and heat are produced.

When heat demands decrease, the pellet factory is started up. In this way, the steam flow in the cogeneration unit is kept at an even level. As a result, the electrical efficiency of the **turbine** stays high, because it falls with any drop in the steam flow. This greater efficiency means the plant can generate as much as 2.5 more megawatts of electricity.

Most of the pellets produced are sold to existing cogeneration plants as a substitute for coal. They are also sold to small heating plants and to **consumers.** Pellets are much easier than wood for the consumer to store and handle.

This power station in Sweden generates energy by burning waste materials rather than **fossil fuels.**

Micro cogeneration plants

Small-scale cogeneration plants that use **internal combustion engines** to burn liquid **petroleum** gas or natural gas can be used to provide energy for office buildings, hospitals, and neighborhoods. These plants usually have outputs of around 15 kilowatts of electricity and 25 kilowatts of heat. A cogeneration plant now provides heat and light to the European Parliament building in Brussels.

Solar Energy

The Sun's energy powers practically all life on Earth and keeps the planet warm enough for that life to exist. Until recently, however, we have lacked a way to tap into this energy and to put it to practical use.

Energy in abundance

Only about one two-billionth of the Sun's energy output reaches Earth. If we could find a way to capture it, even that tiny amount would supply all the world's energy needs. Every day, the Sun generates more energy than all six billion people on Earth use in about 30 years.

Solar thermal collectors

One method of capturing **solar energy** involves using solar thermal collectors. These are heat-absorbing black solar panels placed on some rooftops. Flat plate collectors absorb solar energy and change it to **heat energy**. Water circulates through the panels, where the heat energy is transferred to it. The water is then stored in tanks. Solar water heating is growing in popularity as the price of its technology decreases.

Solar thermal collectors can also be used to produce electricity. The panels use the Sun's rays to produce enough energy to turn water into steam. The steam is then used to run **turbines** to generate electricity, just as it is in a conventional power station.

A solar power station looks nothing like a conventional power station. This picture shows photovoltaic cells in a California desert.

Photovoltaic cells

AT&T's Bell Laboratories invented **photovoltaic cells** in 1954. They eventually were used to power satellites and space vehicles. Today, they not only provide power for satellites, but they also provide electricity and heat water for homes and businesses around the world. Paired with other **renewable energy** sources, such as wind and water, photovoltaic cells can provide energy for entire homes—even entire communities.

Photovoltaic cells power many calculators and all solar-powered cars. They are made of **silicon** and other materials, and change the Sun's rays directly into electricity.

Battery banks

A major problem with solar power is that it is available only during daylight. If we want solar electricity at night, we must find a way to store it during the day. Small machines, such as portable computers, can be powered by batteries that are recharged in daylight by using photovoltaic cells.

If large electric motors used to run a building's air-conditioning system or to run elevators used solar power, they would need large battery banks to run at night or on cloudy days. When the Sun is hidden, a battery bank would have to discharge power. When the Sun was shining, the battery banks would discharge less power as more solar energy became available. Around noon, the photovoltaic cells would begin to produce more energy than needed and would begin recharging the batteries. The batteries would continue to charge throughout the daylight hours. The battery bank is a critical part of solar-powered building. Already, battery banks have been developed that can supply power throughout five days of cloudy weather.

Solar Developments

The day may come when our homes, schools, and workplaces are heated by **solar energy** and when most of our machines are solar-powered. Solar energy is clean, safe, and plentiful. However, it would be a big step to go from the solar-powered pocket calculator to an entirely solar-powered office building.

Scientists and electrical engineers are looking for ways to make better and cheaper **photovoltaic cells.** One way to do this is to develop materials that are more transparent, or see-through. For example, scientists have developed new **silicon** parts that do not prevent the Sun's rays from hitting the light-sensitive metal part of the cell. Smaller, more light-sensitive cells will capture more sunlight, and therefore provide more energy.

Designing solar cells

The solar power industry is working on ways to improve its technology. It is also looking at how to use the technology in the structure of buildings. For example, roofing tiles or shingles can now be replaced by rows of solar cells. Designers can use clear panels in office buildings.

Eventually, more modern glass and steel skyscrapers in cities could have large solar panels instead of glass. Designers are manufacturing solar panels in different colors and shapes. As a result, a building's power source could become part of the building's design.

Solar communications

Hundreds of pay phones in remote parts of Australia now run on solar power. In addition, the houses in which athletes lived for the 2000 Sydney Olympics were designed to run largely on solar power.

Solar homes

Although solar power is used primarily to support or back up conventional sources of power, there are already about 20,000 homes across the United States that totally rely on solar power. The reason there are not more solar-powered homes is that solar power equipment costs around three to five times as much as getting power from the local utility companies. However, it may be worth it for people who live in remote areas. It might also be worthwhile for rural communities in countries in which the electricity supply is not as efficient as it is in the industrialized nations.

A Million Solar Roofs

In 1997, President Bill Clinton announced the Million Solar Roofs campaign. By 2010, the U.S. government hopes to have solar energy systems installed on one million buildings throughout the United States and, in the process, create 70,000 new jobs. The U.S. Department of Energy expects the solar energy market to earn more than $1.5 billion worldwide within the next few years.

Many of the Sydney Olympic Stadium buildings used solar panels to generate power.

Blowing in the Wind

Wind power is related to **solar energy** because it is the energy of the Sun that powers Earth's weather systems and makes the wind blow. People have used the power of wind for hundreds of years to grind grain, pump water, and sail ships. Wind **turbines** were first used to generate electricity during the 1900s. During the next few decades, wind power may supply a significant part of our energy needs.

Wind into electricity

Turning wind into electricity is fairly simple. Rotor blades, rather like aircraft propellers, are mounted on a tower in a windy location. The wind spins the blades, which are linked to the shaft of an electricity **generator.** The generator then produces electricity, which is carried by power lines to wherever it is needed. Wind turbines can be used singly or in groups known as wind farms. The wind turbines used in a wind farm are usually about 185 feet (60 meters) tall. Other wind turbines can be much smaller. These are often called wind chargers, because they are used to charge large batteries. Wind chargers can be used to provide power for homes with no other electricity supply.

Although it seems easy to generate, wind power has not been used very much. The main reason for this is cost. It costs a lot of money to build several hundred full-size turbines. During the early 1980s, wind-generated electricity was up to three times more expensive than power from **fossil fuels.** By the early 1990s, however, new designs had made wind power more affordable.

The energy of the wind powers this yacht. Wind is a natural resource.

Today, the United States is the leading **consumer** of wind power in the world. In Europe, several countries are rapidly developing wind energy as they look for ways to lower their dependence on fossil fuels and **nuclear energy** and lessen pollution. People in remote areas in developing nations have bought many small wind turbines in order to bring power to small villages.

The right site

The most important thing that determines how effective a wind farm will be is its location. Most wind farms are in places where the wind is strongest, such as North Dakota and California in the United States, and Wales, Scotland, and Cornwall in Great Britain. One of the biggest problems is that wind farms take up large areas of land. Land is valuable, especially in small, crowded countries, such as Britain. However, this difficulty can be overcome if wind farms are put on land used for other purposes, such as farming. For a wind farm to work well, wind speed is not as important as one might think. But the wind must blow steadily. If the wind blows for an hour or less a day, it will not be enough to generate power.

This wind farm is in Altamont Pass, California.

No one is sure just how important wind power could be. One study estimated that around half of the United States's electricity needs could be met by wind farms scattered around the country's windiest areas. Even if that estimate proves to be unrealistic, it does seem that wind power has great potential.

Ocean breezes

Scientists are looking into ways to set up wind farms in the ocean, where strong winds blow more consistently. To harness this offshore wind power, the bases of the wind turbines would have to be fixed firmly to the ocean floor. The turbines would have to be strong enough to withstand ocean storms. Turbines like these are already in use by Britain and Denmark.

25

Hydroelectricity

Hydroelectric power is generated from the **kinetic energy** of moving water, a powerful and **renewable energy** source. About four percent of the world's energy needs are met in this way, but some scientists estimate that about twenty percent of our energy needs could be met if all suitable sites were used. Like many other sources of renewable energy, hydroelectricity is a clean source of power and does not produce air pollution. In addition, once the huge initial costs of constructing a dam and power station have been taken care of, hydropower is inexpensive.

Hydroelectricity generated by the Grand Coulee Dam in the state of Washington is a renewable source of energy.

Hydro-history

The power of running water was first harnessed using water wheels placed in rivers. There, the currents caught their large blades and made them spin. The Romans used water wheels to move grindstones to mill their grain. During the 1600s and 1700s, rivers and streams were dammed and redirected throughout Europe. People used water energy for grinding wheat and other cereals, to pump water from wells, and to power spinning wheels and other textile equipment.

Hydroelectric dams

At the end of the 1800s, people found a new way of using water—the hydroelectric dam. It was far better at capturing the energy of rushing water than water wheels were. Today, the most common form of hydroelectric power involves building dams on rivers. This creates large reservoirs of water that can be directed through concrete troughs and pipes to **turbines,** making them spin. The turbines are connected to electricity **generators.**

The taller a dam, the more energy it can produce. This is because the higher the water, the greater its **potential energy.** Well over 100 dams around the world are over 490 feet (150 meters) tall. The highest in the world is the Rogun Dam in Russia, which is more than 1,000 feet (335 meters) tall.

Mountainous countries such as the United States, Canada, and Norway are the best places to make use of hydroelectric power. There are more than 2,000 hydroelectric power stations in the United States, and most of the rivers that could be used for hydroelectricity have been dammed. Spain and Italy get more than a third of their electricity from hydroelectric power. Canada gets two-thirds of its electricity from this source and exports a great deal of it to the United States.

Falling from favor

In recent years, environmentalists have discouraged the use of hydroelectricity because it can hurt the environment. Damming rivers can change the **ecology** of a region because whole areas become flooded. The water below a dam is often colder than it would be normally, and this can harm fish. Changing water levels can harm plants that grow along the riverbanks. Hydroelectric power, which was once seen as a clean and limitless source of energy, has a downside just as **fossil fuels** do. However, so-called "micro-hydro" installations might be a solution. They are small-scale installations that have little impact on the ecology of a region.

Many people, such as this group in India, fight against the use of hydroelectric power because it can have negative effects.

Wave Power

If put to use, the waves in the ocean can create a tremendous amount of energy. When wind hits the water, it transfers massive amounts of **potential energy** to the water. The best way to capture some of this energy is the **oscillating** water column (OWC). When waves of water hit an OWC, the air inside is compressed and forced through air **turbines.**

As waves crash against a shore, you can see how much energy they carry.

The first successful OWC device was used in Japan to power a light on the top of a navigation buoy. OWCs are still mostly experimental, but one is already in use in Tofteshallen, Norway. It is one of the most advanced wave-to-energy devices in the world, creating 500 kilowatts of electricity. A device being developed by a group of European companies works on the same principles.

Ducks and buoys

Wave-powered **generators** would have to be sturdy enough to withstand the changeable and sometimes rough conditions at sea. In 1974, British designer Stephen Salter developed the "duck," a floating **boom** that got its name because the segments bob up and down like a duck as the waves pass. The nodding motion can be used to spin generators to produce electricity.

While the device is still at an experimental stage, it appears that it will generate electricity more efficiently than has been done before from wave power. It is a free-floating buoy, which means that it can move with the waves and therefore better withstand storm conditions. Devices like this could be used to supply power to remote islands and offshore oil rigs.

The world's first commercial wave-powered electricity generator was launched on the Clyde River in Scotland in 1995. The plant, called Osprey, was expected to generate 2 megawatts of electricity from wave power and 1.5 megawatts from a wind turbine. Unfortunately, it failed a few weeks after launch.

Ocean thermal energy

The temperature of the ocean is different at different depths, and this offers another possible way to generate power from the oceans. **Heat energy** moves from the hotter parts of the ocean to the colder parts. If this heat is channeled through a heat-powered engine, it can be used to generate electricity.

This process, which is called ocean thermal energy conversion, might be a good energy source for island nations such as those in the Pacific Ocean. But the technology required is expensive, and many of the countries that would benefit from it are poor. So far, there has been little research on how this technology would affect the environment.

Tidal Energy

Tidal energy is a **renewable energy** source that is powered by the force of **gravity.** The idea of using the energy of the tides is not new. Tidal mills were built in Britain, France, and Spain as early as the 1100s. These early mills produced the equivalent of 20 to 75 kilowatts of power, which is less than the power available in a modern car.

This is the original La Rance tidal mill showing the sluice, or flood gates and tidal pool.

There are not that many places in the world where the tidal range, or the difference between high tide and and low tide, is large enough to justify the use of tidal energy. To make a tidal power station worthwhile, there must be a tidal range of at least 16 feet (5 meters).

The world's most powerful tides occur in the Bay of Fundy in Canada, where tidal ranges of up to 55 feet (17 meters) are common. The United States, Britain, France, northwest Australia, Argentina, Brazil, India, and Russia all have stretches of coastline with tidal ranges large enough to support tidal power. The total capacity of all potential tidal-power sites in the world has been estimated to be about one billion kilowatts. The world's first tidal power station, in La Rance, France, can produce enough power to provide for the energy needs of around 300,000 people.

Tidal technology

The ocean can be used to generate power in several ways. For example, a dam could be built across a cove or an **estuary** with a large tidal range. The dam would consist of a powerhouse, a **sluiceway** or floodgate section, and a solid embankment. When the tide comes in, the sluiceways are opened, and the area behind the dam fills with water. At high tide, the sluiceway gates are closed.

The trapped water is allowed to return to the ocean through pipes, spinning electricity-generating **turbines** as it does so. It is possible to install turbines that can generate electricity in both directions, both as the tide ebbs and as it flows. When the tide begins to turn and the water level rises again, the sluiceways are opened again. The dammed area fills up, ready for the next cycle of electrical generation.

Time and tide

The average electricity output from tidal power is limited by the twice daily ebb and flow of the tides. The average output of electricity from a tidal plant is less than 40 percent of its potential generating capacity, because it is only generating electricity half the time. On the other hand, the production of power from **hydroelectric** power stations averages between 70 and 100 percent of capacity.

This is the La Rance tidal power station in Brittany, France.

Another problem is that the tides are powered by the gravitational pull of the Moon. The lunar cycle of 24 hours and 50 minutes means that the production of tidal energy does not match the demand for energy 24 hours a day. In other words, the tidal power station may not be performing to capacity when demand for power is greatest. So the tidal energy must be either stored or used with other sources of power to make sure that power is there when needed.

Tidal power stations may not be able to replace conventional **fossil fuel** stations, but they can work alongside them. The use of the fossil-fueled stations can be cut back when the tidal plant begins to generate power. It can be increased again during the few hours that a tidal plant must stay idle because there is not enough water flow. As a result, we can conserve our coal and oil reserves and decrease pollution.

Geothermal Energy

The term *geothermal* means "heat from Earth." Sources of **geothermal energy** are widespread. They include the hot water and hot rock found a few miles beneath Earth's surface, and the extremely high temperatures of molten rock called magma found at deeper levels. The best features of geothermal energy are that it is generally non-polluting and it is renewable.

Geothermal pumps

Geothermal pumps make use of the fact that the top 10 feet (3 meters) of Earth's surface maintains a nearly constant temperature—between 45 and 60° F (10 and 15° C). A geothermal heat pump system is made up of a heat pump, an air delivery system, and a heat exchanger, which is a system of pipes buried in the shallow ground near the building. During winter, the heat pump removes heat from the heat exchanger and pumps it into the indoor air delivery system, warming the inside of the building. In the summer months, the process is reversed. The indoor air temperature is greater than the shallow ground temperature, and the heat pump moves heat from the indoor air into the heat exchanger. The heat removed from the indoor air can also be used to provide a free source of hot water.

Geothermal reservoirs

Heat rising from molten magma several miles beneath the surface warms underground pools of water known as geothermal reservoirs. Sometimes, the water is heated enough for it to boil and turn to steam. If there are openings through the rock to the surface, the hot water may seep out to form hot springs, or it may erupt out in the form of a geyser.

Geothermal power stations, like this one in northern California, can generate as much electricity as conventional power stations.

Hot water near the surface of Earth is used for heating buildings, growing plants in greenhouses, heating water at fish farms, and purifying milk. Wells can tap directly into geothermal reservoirs and pump the water to the surface. This is called direct use of geothermal energy. Geothermal power plants can use steam directly from a reservoir to power a **turbine**.

The Geysers geothermal field located in northern California is the largest source of geothermal energy in the world. It produces as much power as two large coal or nuclear power plants.

Hot dry rocks

Hot dry rock resources occur at depths of three to five miles (five to eight kilometers) everywhere beneath Earth's surface. In areas where there is volcanic activity, they will be nearer to the surface. Getting energy from these resources involves injecting cold water down one well, circulating it through the hot fractured rock, and then taking the heated water from another well. Today, this technology is not being used, and there is no way to recover heat directly from magma. Even though magma is the most powerful resource of geothermal energy, it lies too deep underground. It reaches Earth's surface only during volcanic eruptions.

A volcanic eruption reveals the tremendous energy hidden within Earth.

Drawbacks of geothermal energy

Although geothermal energy is a clean and reliable source of power, it is not readily available to everyone. People either do not live near a geothermal reservoir, or they lack the technology to use the shallow ground energy. It might also be possible that by using it, so much water could be drawn out of a reservoir that it could not replenish itself. In addition, water from geothermal reservoirs often contains minerals that cause pollution.

Biomass Energy

For hundreds of thousands of years, people have used wood, charcoal, and plant and animal wastes to heat their homes and cook their food. These fuels are called **biomass** fuels, or simply biomass. Today, biomass is used to generate electricity and to produce liquid fuels, such as methanol and **ethanol,** to power vehicles. Biomass fuels are an important energy source, especially in developing countries. Homes, farms, and factories produce wastes of all kinds that could be used as biomass fuel.

Bioelectric power

The biggest advances in biomass technology will probably be in the field of electricity production. Parts of the timber industry are already burning wood and paper wastes to produce steam to drive electric **generators.** However, many people believe that **biogas turbines** would be a more efficient way to tap into this energy source. Biomass can be easily changed into methane, a fuel that can power gas turbines. Eighty countries in the developing world produce sugar cane, a crop that generates much waste material. Some people believe that this waste could be changed into biogas that would generate up to 40 percent of the electricity needed by rural communities in these countries.

A great deal of this Brazilian sugar cane crop is waste material that could be used to make **biofuels.**

Biomass is more readily available and causes less pollution than **fossil fuels.** For example, biomass may contain one thirtieth the amount of sulfur and produce one fifth of the amount of ash that is produced by some types of coal. However, like fossil fuels, biomass produces carbon dioxide when it is burned. Carbon dioxide is one of the materials plants use during **photosynthesis,** and the amount produced when biomass is burned is the same as what the plant took in when it was growing. In theory,

In India, many people change plant and animal waste into useful fuel using biogas digesters like this one.

therefore, as long as new biomass fuel is being grown as quickly as it is being used, the carbon dioxide levels in the atmosphere should not be affected by burning biomass fuels.

Biofuel production

Biomass is the only practical source of renewable liquid fuel, so scientists are looking for ways to produce economical liquid fuels from biomass. In the past, research has focused on producing ethanol from corn. Growing corn can be expensive, however, because it requires large amounts of energy, **fertilizers,** pesticides, and water to grow.

Energy from scraps

According to the U.S. Department of Energy, biomass is currently supplying as much energy as a billion barrels of oil per year in the United States. Most of this energy comes from electricity generated by the burning of sawdust and wood scraps from lumber mills.

An alternative method to produce fuel is to use fast- growing trees. Researchers try to identify the fastest-growing variety of tree in a region, so that it can be bred with other trees to produce a tree that grows even faster. Green wood can be changed into methanol, which can be used directly in a vehicle or changed to high-**octane** gasoline. The only by-product is wood ash, and this can be used as fertilizer.

Biomass Pros and Cons

Biomass fuel is bulky and difficult to transport. It takes about three tons of wood to produce the same amount of energy as a ton of coal. Even so, using biomass fuel to generate electricity is still practical if the fuel is used close to where it is produced. In the pulp, paper, and timber industry in North America, for example, wood chips and paper scraps are burned to generate electricity for the factories that produce paper products.

When properly conserved, trees are a valuable and renewable source of energy and materials.

In rural parts of Asia, water buffalo manure is dried for heating and cooking fuel. **Biogas generators** in China produce methane, mostly from pig manure. One problem with using dung as fuel is that it could decrease the amounts available for **fertilizer**, at the same time that the plants being grown for fuel are taking valuable nutrients from the soil.

Some environmentalists are against biomass crops because the crops are monocultures—crops that are all of the same species. Monocultures are more vulnerable to pests, which encourages the use of pesticides. Also, a natural disaster, such as a drought, would be particularly bad in any region relying heavily on biomass fuels. It would deprive them of both their food and their energy supply. On the plus side, biomass crops can be grown on unused fields, creating more income for farmers.

Pollution control

In 1992, waste-to-energy combustor plants, or the plants that produce biomass energy, in the United States produced the same amount of energy as 30 million barrels of oil. This biomass is not as clean as wood, however. Pollution-control devices have to be fitted to combustor plants so they do not give off harmful substances into the environment.

Biomass potential

It is clear that biomass has the potential to replace some of the **fossil fuels** now used to power small vehicles. It could also replace some of the fossil fuels that are burned to generate electricity. But these changes will not come about until car manufacturers greatly improve the fuel economy of their cars and engineers build more efficient gas **turbine** units.

Biomass technology could lower carbon dioxide emissions. Although some carbon dioxide is given off when biomass is burned, it is less than what is given off when fossil fuels are burned. It has been estimated that if countries would achieve their biomass production potential, carbon dioxide levels could be cut in half. However, this would require huge areas of land for growing fuel.

Energy harvest

One of the biggest advantages of biomass is that it is **renewable.** The thirty years or so it takes for a tree to mature are a lot fewer than the millions of years it takes for coal to form. If a biomass crop is managed carefully, making sure that it is harvested at the same it is replanted, it is possible to maintain a biomass crop.

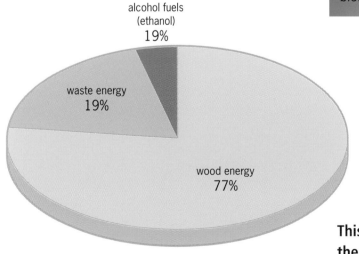

alcohol fuels
(ethanol)
19%

waste energy
19%

wood energy
77%

This pie chart shows the biomass energy used in the United States in 1997.

Neighborhood Concerns

Every alternative source of energy has some impact on the environment. Take wind power, for example. The wind itself is invisible, but a 20-foot (60-meter) tall wind **turbine** is difficult to avoid. Few people want a wind farm next door to their homes. The whirling rotors are also a danger to birds. A study at Altamont Pass, a region of California in which several medium-sized turbines have been built, showed that about 100 birds of prey had been killed by the spinning blades during a three-and-a-half-year period.

Drawbacks to hydroelectric power

There is no escaping the fact that dams drastically alter the **ecology** of nearby land and water habitats. Upstream from a dam, river life finds itself in what has become a lake. It may find it hard to adapt to the new conditions. Downstream, changes in the height, speed, and temperature of the flowing water can also harm river life.

Between 1950 and 1975, India lost 480,000 acres (194,000 hectares) of forest when waters were backed up behind new dams. In the Pacific Northwest of the United States, some dams block the annual migration routes of Pacific salmon, preventing them from reaching their breeding areas upstream. At least three species of salmon have become endangered or threatened because of **hydroelectric** dams.

The land on the banks of the Nile is very fertile. People have been farming there for thousands of years.

Hydroelectric dams can affect people, too, because the dams interfere with natural cycles of erosion and flooding. For example, along the Nile River in Egypt, annual floods had for centuries swept over nearby fields. These floods deposited a layer of nutrient-rich sediment that had been loosened from banks and plains upstream. After the Aswan High Dam blocked the Nile's flow in 1970, the seasonal floods stopped. As a result, the fields became so unproductive that Egyptian farmers had to start buying artificial **fertilizers.**

Drawbacks to geothermal energy

There are definite drawbacks to **geothermal energy,** too. As scientists look for sources of geothermal energy, they might have to build roads in wilderness areas, just as they do during oil exploration. Such construction work can disturb the local ecology. Noise from construction work and the operation of the geothermal plants can scare animals away. In Hawaii, for example, a geothermal development has destroyed parts of that area's last undeveloped tropical rainforest.

Mineral-rich geothermal waters are disposed of after they are cooled. If they are emptied into lakes or streams, they may harm organisms that live there. The minerals in the waste water may also cause weeds to spread, clogging waterways and preventing oxygen from reaching the water. Hydrogen sulfide gas, which smells like rotten eggs, often rises from geothermal sites. **Acid rain** forms when hydrogen sulfide is oxidized to make sulfur dioxide,which combines with water to form sulfuric acid.

Geothermal sites also give off carbon dioxide, one of the **greenhouse gases.** However, coal- or oil-fired power plants producing the same amount of energy give off much more.

All geothermal power plants have an impact on the environment.

39

The Alternative Future

There is no escaping the fact that we have become very energy demanding, surrounding ourselves with many power-hungry gadgets. Many people in developing countries want to own these gadgets, too. If we are to have sustainable energy in the future, we need to balance how much energy we use and how much we produce. Technical solutions, as well as social and political solutions, are needed.

In 1971, the world used an amount of energy equal to 4,722 million tons of oil. About 97 percent of this energy was from **fossil fuels**. Just 20 years later, energy use was up to 7,074 million tons. Of this, 90 percent was from fossil fuels. The seven percent decrease was due to nuclear power. By 2010, energy consumption is expected to rise to the equivalent of 11,500 million tons, with fossil fuels still accounting for 90 percent.

The oil industry continues to discover new oil deposits by developing more effective methods of oil exploration. Improved technology allows oil companies to take oil from places that were previously inaccessible, such as deep-water sites. But this does not change the fact that fossil fuels are a limited, nonrenewable resource that cannot meet the world's increasing demands for energy. Sustaining our energy supply may not seem important today, but it will be for our descendants.

The polar icecaps are melting. Carbon dioxide emissions are suspected as the cause of this problem.

Energy and economics

The driving force behind most technological developments has been the desire to make money. Car manufacturers, for example, will make environmentally friendly cars only if people want to buy them. The electric car was doomed because nobody wanted it. It was just too inconvenient to run. On the other hand, everyone can understand the benefits of fuel efficiency and getting more for their money, and people will happily buy a car that goes farther for less.

We will continue to rely on fossil fuels for our energy needs for as long as possible because there is nothing as cheap and efficient as coal, oil, and gas. Sixty-four percent of the world's electricity supply is generated by burning fossil fuels; eighteen percent comes from **hydroelectric** power; seventeen percent comes from nuclear power; and less than one percent comes from all the other sources discussed in this book, including **geothermal**, **biomass**, wind, tidal, and solar power. Nuclear power is becoming less popular, and its use is expected to go down over the next few decades.

If we are to have a sustainable energy supply, we have to learn to value people over power. We have to stop living only in the present and start thinking about the future—not just our own future, but the future of all the people who come after us. Fortunately, there are some signs that we might just do that.

The hydroelectric power plant at Niagara Falls, New York, produces about 1,950 megawatts of electricity.

Saving for the Future

More and more companies in the developed nations are changing the way they heat and light their buildings. They are doing this not only to lessen **greenhouse gas** emissions, but also to lower their energy bills. The reductions they achieve often exceed those called for in the 1997 Kyoto Treaty, an international agreement about greenhouse warming. The treaty's goal is to lower greenhouse gas emissions to seven percent below the 2000 levels. This is being accomplished despite the fact that many U.S. oil, coal, and chemicals companies complained that the Kyoto Treaty was a threat to the country's economy.

Companies are realizing that being environmentally responsible can save, and not cost, money. The Royal Dutch/Shell Company, for example, is aiming to lower greenhouse-gas emissions at its plants to 25 percent below 1990 levels by 2002. The DuPont Pharmaceutical Company aims to cut its greenhouse emissions by 40 percent from its 1991 levels. Boeing Aircraft Company upgraded its lighting and lowered its use of electricity for lighting by 90 percent. This means that about 100,000 fewer tons of carbon dioxide enter the atmosphere every year.

The Boeing Aircraft Company is saving a lot of energy simply because of having upgraded its lighting.

Developing needs

Many energy planners believe that if we are to meet world energy needs, we should consider alternative energy sources in light of the following criteria:

- Their suitability to particular places. For example, Switzerland may have the potential for wind and **hydroelectric** power, but it would be inefficient to transport energy from wave **generators** within this small country.
- Their environmental and health risks. Renewable sources do not give off the kinds of air pollutants that burning fuels do, but they do raise other environmental issues. It is unrealistic to expect that a power source can be 100 percent safe. But how close do we have to get to be happy to use it?
- Who will pay to research and develop different alternative energy sources? For example, some alternative energy sources may be most useful in developing nations that cannot afford to take advantage of them. Should industrial nations help pay for these technologies, or should each country be expected to develop its own sources? In addition, many developing countries have large coal resources. Should they be forbidden to develop them?
- How can the many different sources of alternative energy be combined into a global system that will make the best use of the strengths and minimize the drawbacks of each?

The price to pay

For many people, energy efficiency is only attractive if it saves money in the short term. They may ask, for example, whether it is cheaper to buy insulating material for the house or to buy extra fuel to heat it. However, a more important question is whether the short-term savings is worth a huge environmental price in the future.

People do not always focus on long-term effects when making decisions. There are few politicians, for example, who are prepared to make unpopular decisions, such as introducing taxes on carbon fuels, or raising motor vehicle taxes to cut back on carbon dioxide pollution. While insulating material might cost a little more now, your grandchildren might be grateful that you did not burn that extra fuel.

Alternative Energy Statistics

Top ten hydroelectricity producers
(in billion kilowatthours)

Canada	340
United States	306
Brazil	306
China	223
Russia	158
Norway	120
Japan	85
India	81
Sweden	72
France	69

Top ten wind energy producers
(in megawatts: one megawatt = 1 million watts)

Germany	3,817
United States	2,533
Denmark	1,606
Spain	1,180
India	1,032
Netherlands	405
United Kingdom	350
China	246
Italy	227
Sweden	197

How much energy is alternative energy?

(figures are a percentage of the total energy use in Europe)

Hydroelectric Energy

Pluses: well-established technology; large **hydroelectric** plants can generate a lot of power (300 to 400 megawatts); no carbon dioxide emissions

Minuses: environmental damage caused by dam building; lack of suitable sites

2000: 13%

2010: 12.4%

Wind Energy

Pluses: technology is improving with individual machines capable of generating 3 megawatts being developed; no carbon dioxide emissions

Minuses: turbines are noisy and unsightly; lack of suitable sites; wind does not blow continually; turbines can harm, or even kill, birds

2000: 0.2%

2010: 2.8%

Photovoltaic/Solar Energy

Pluses: completely **renewable energy** source; can be used anywhere; no carbon dioxide emission

Minuses: requires a large area to generate much power; technology is expensive (although prices are falling)

2000: 0.03%

2010: 0.1%

Fuel-cell Energy

Pluses: could replace **internal combustion engines** as a power source for cars; no carbon dioxide emissions

Minuses: require **fossil fuels** to produce the hydrogen fuel; expensive technology at present

2000: 0%

2010: 0%

Biomass Energy

Pluses: plentiful sources in wastes from agriculture and forestry; a renewable fuel; established technology

Minuses: creates pollution, including carbon dioxide emissions; expensive to collect, transport, and store **biomass**

2000: 0.95%

2010: 8%

Glossary

acid rain rain that contains sulfur dioxide from coal burning and nitrogen oxides from car exhausts and other sources

atom smallest unit of matter that can take part in a chemical reaction; smallest part of an element that can exist

biofuel fuel from living material, such as wood

biogas fuel produced by fermenting living material

biomass organic matter, such as wood and other plant materials and animal wastes

boom floating beam used to form a barrier over the surface of water

chemical energy energy in the bonds that hold atoms together in molecules that is given off during a chemical reaction

cogeneration combined heat and power

consumer someone who buys and uses goods or services

ecology relationships between living things and their environment and the study of these relationships

estuary water passage in which a tide meets a river current

ethanol ethyl alcohol, which can be used as a fuel

fertilizer chemical or natural substance added to soil to provide nutrients

fossil fuel fuel produced through the action of heat and pressure on the fossil remains of plants and animals that lived millions of years ago

fuel cell device similar to a battery that changes chemical energy into electrical energy

generator machine that produces electrical energy from mechanical energy

geothermal energy energy taken from the hot rocks and water beneath Earth's surface

global warming rise in the average temperature of Earth over recent years, which some people blame on increasing levels of greenhouse gases, like carbon dioxide, in the atmosphere; other people think it may be a natural climate change

gravity force of attraction at the surface of a planet

greenhouse gas gas in the atmosphere, such as carbon dioxide or methane, that prevents heat radiated from Earth's surface from escaping into space

heat energy energy created by moving atoms and molecules

hybrid something made by combining two different things and having some qualities of both

hydride compound of hydrogen and any other element

hydroelectric/hydroelectricity relating to the production of electricity using the energy of flowing water

insulate prevent the passage of heat or electricity

internal combustion engine engine in which the fuel is burned inside the device

kinetic energy energy of movement

microorganism living thing that is too small to be seen without a microscope

molecule two or more atoms joined by chemical bonds; if the atoms are the same, it is an element; if they are different, it is a compound

natural gas substance often found along with petroleum deposits within layers of sedimentary rock that can be used as fuel; including methane, propane, and butane

nuclear energy energy in the nucleus of an atom given off when a large nucleus breaks into two smaller nuclei or when two small nuclei form a larger nucleus

nuclear fusion process by which two small atomic nuclei combine to produce a single larger nucleus while giving off a large amount of energy

octane measure of the properties of petroleum fuel

OPEC Organization of Petroleum Exporting Countries; intergovernmental organization that oversees the petroleum policies of its members

oscillate move back and forth at a regular speed

petroleum thick, liquid mixture found underground, formed by the action of bacteria and the forces of high pressure and temperature on the remains of marine plants and animals over millions of years

photosynthesis process by which green plants and some other organisms use the energy of the Sun to make sugars from carbon dioxide and water

photovoltaic cell device that changes light energy into electrical energy

potential energy energy stored within a system because of its position or state

recycle to change waste into material that can be used

renewable energy energy from a source that can be restored; most such sources (wind, tides, waves) can be traced back to the energy of the Sun

silicon chemical element with properties that make it invaluable to the electronics industry

sluiceway opening to a dam

solar energy energy from the Sun

synthetic made artificially

turbine engine in which a fluid is used to spin a shaft by pushing on angled blades; used to spin electricity generators

More Books to Read

Graham, Ian. *Solar Power.* Austin, Tex.: Raintree Steck-Vaughn, 1999.

Graham, Ian. *Wind Power.* Austin, Tex.: Raintree Steck-Vaughn, 1999.

Oxlade, Chris. *Energy.* Chicago: Heinemann Library, 1999.

Snedden, Robert. *Energy.* Chicago: Heinemann Library, 1999.

Index

Energy alternatives /
J 333.79 SNEDD   31057001168890

Snedden, Robert.
WEST GA REGIONAL LIBRARY SYS